Biographies of famous people to
support the curriculum.

William
Shakespeare

by Emma Fischel
Illustrations by Martin Remphrey

FRANKLIN WATTS
NEW YORK•LONDON•SYDNEY

First published in 1998 by
Franklin Watts
96 Leonard Street
London
EC2A 4RH

Franklin Watts Australia
14 Mars Road
Lane Cove
NSW 2066

ISBN: 0 7496 2895 2

A CIP catalogue record for this book
is available from the British Library.

Dewey Decimal Classification Number: 822.3

10 9 8 7 6 5 4 3

Series editor: Sarah Ridley
Series designer: Kirstie Billingham
Consultant: Dr Anne Millard

Printed in Great Britain

William Shakespeare

William Shakespeare is the
most famous English writer ever
– and probably the most famous
writer in the whole world.
He wrote poetry and plays,
(stories to be acted on a stage).

William lived over four hundred
years ago. But even now visitors
from all over the world come
every day to see where he
was born.

They can see lots of other things
too, like the school he went to
and the church he is buried in.

And almost every day they
can see William's plays, put on
in special theatres built in
his honour.

ROYAL SHAKESPEARE
THEATRE

SHAKESPEARE'S
SCHOOL

SHAKESPEARE'S
FAMILY
HOUSE.

When William was born
Mr and Mrs Shakespeare were
very happy...

Our first boy!

but very worried.

Their first two babies hadn't
lived long. Babies often died
very young then, as there were
not many medicines.

A horrible disease called the plague was killing lots of people. Would baby William die too? Luckily William survived and so did the next five babies.

In those days many children worked to earn money for their families, instead of going to school.

William's family was quite well off, though. His father was an important man in Stratford. So William went to school.

8

Schools were only for boys –
and they were tough places.
Most of the teachers were
tough too.

When William was young, people in towns put on plays based on bible stories each summer.

There were no theatres then so groups of actors performed their plays anywhere they could.

Then, one day, exciting news came to Stratford.

Hear Ye! First theatre opens in London.

No one knew it then, but that theatre would be the first of many. William was growing up at just the right time!

Sad times hit the Shakespeare family. William's sister Anne died when he was fifteen. She was only eight.

Things went badly wrong with his father's work, too.

That changed things for William.
"I can no longer stay at school,"
he said. "I must find work!"

No one knows exactly what he
did next – but he had plenty
of choices.

One thing we DO know is that when William was eighteen he fell in love with Anne Hathaway.

They married and soon had a baby. Then two years later they had another two!

And they all lived in the house
William had grown up in, along
with all the other Shakespeares.

Another theatre opened in London, then another. More and more plays were being written too – and not just based on stories from the Bible.

William made a decision.
"I must leave Stratford," he said.
"London is the place to be!"

London was the biggest city in
the whole of England. It was
quite different from Stratford.

William was now twenty-three.
He soon found work as an actor.

Most actors stuck to playing one
kind of part in those days.
William wasn't sure yet what he
was best at.

The actors often helped to write
the plays as well, or changed
the words while they rehearsed.

THAT was when William found
out what he was really good at.

William watched other writers'
plays as well. He listened and
he learned.

He talked to other writers and
actors about what they thought
made plays good or bad. He
didn't always agree with them.

But it all helped him work out
what kind of plays he wanted
to write.

It was an exciting time in
England then.

The English had
a clever queen
on the throne,
and more
money too.
They were doing well!

A huge fleet of
ships from Spain,
called the Armada,
tried to conquer
England but was
soon chased off.

HENRY VI
PART 1 1589

Brave explorers sailed around the world, bringing back stories of new lands they had found.

It all gave William ideas as he started work on his first play.

BATTLES!

HEROES!

SUCCESS!

ICTORIES!

William was nervous. What if
no one liked his plays?

Theatres were different then.
The audience stood all round
the stage. And they made it very
clear if they didn't like what
they saw...

William didn't need to worry
though. The audiences only had
one thing to say about his plays.

People watched a lot of violent things in those days, like bear baiting, where bears were chained up then attacked by vicious dogs.

Criminals were hung or beheaded in public too, so everyone could see.

That gave William even more
ideas for his next play.

In the play Titus has his hands
chopped off and his deadly
enemy, Tamora, kills his sons.
Titus kills her sons, cooks them in
a pie and serves them up to her!

By the time William was thirty
he was famous. Most people
thought he was very clever –
but not everyone.

Over the next five years he
wrote some of his most popular
plays. Some were sad, some
were funny...

In *A Midsummer Night's Dream*, Titania, Queen of the fairies, is tricked by magic into falling in love with a poor man wearing a donkey's head.

Lots of different theatre companies put on plays in London then. Each company was owned by a rich person, called a patron.

William soon caught the eye of one of them.

Allow me to introduce myself, the Lord Chamberlain.

William joined his company,
the Chamberlain's Men.

Many people thought their
acting company was the best
in England.

The Chamberlain's Men were a favourite with someone very important indeed - The Queen of England, Queen Elizabeth I!

Elizabeth loved music, poetry – and plays. In fact, she liked one of William's plays so much she had a special request to make.

THE MERRY WIVES OF WINDSOR

"That fat little rogue, Falstaff, in your latest play," she said. "Write me another play specially about him!"

So William did.

William was now writing about
two plays a year in London, but
his family was still in Stratford.
He visited them as often as he
could. He was rich, successful
and tired out.

Then something horrible
happened. William's son, Hamnet,
died. He was only eleven.

A year later William bought a
house in Stratford.

It was a very big house. Only one
house in Stratford was bigger!

Back in London, Richard Burbage had a plan. "Let's build our own theatre!" he said.

"Why not!" said William, and others in the Chamberlain's Men agreed. They all worked together to get it started.

Every ticket they sold made each of them some money – and they sold lots of tickets.

"The Globe is a success," they said. "We're rich."

Now William was writing some
of his most famous plays,
called tragedies.

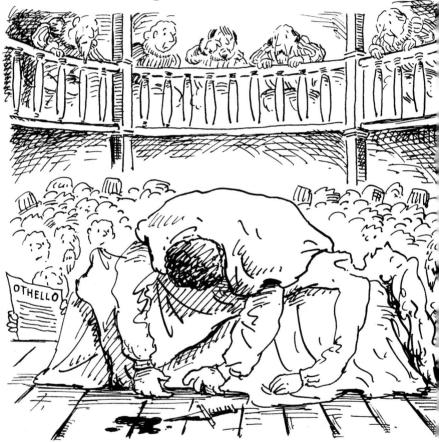

Tragedies were very sad stories
with very sad endings.

William's tragedies made people think about the right and wrong ways to behave. He wrote about important things like good and evil, love and hate. And he made them exciting too.

When William was just over forty, Queen Elizabeth I died. The Scottish king, James VI, became James I of England too.

William wrote his last great tragedy specially for the new king. The play was all about Scotland and Scottish kings. William called it *Macbeth*.

In the play, three witches tell Macbeth he will be king. He kills the real king – and anyone else who gets in his way.

One victim haunts him as a ghost. In the end Macbeth is killed himself.

41

William wrote poems as well as plays. Most of his poems were about love. Some of them were very, very long.

VENUS
AND
ADONIS
PAGE 52

His most famous poems were called sonnets. Each one was fourteen lines long – and he wrote 154 of them.

His poems were very popular at
the royal court.

Now William was nearly fifty.
"It is time to leave London," he
said. He went to live in his house
in Stratford. He died there when
he was fifty-two years old.

He left money to help the poor
people in Stratford. He left
money to his actor friends too.
He asked them to buy rings to
remember him by.

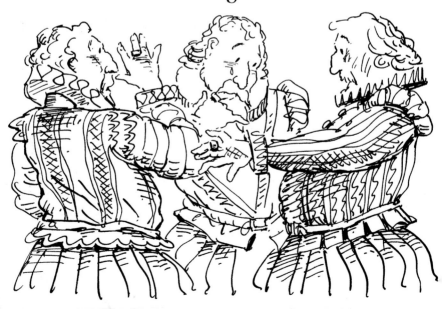

A statue was put up in the church he is buried in. You can still see it there today.

Further facts

About the theatre

There were no women actors in William's time, so their parts were played by boys. In some of William's plays his women characters disguise themselves as men. It all got very complicated for the boy actors!

You are a boy, pretending to be a woman, pretending to be a man. Simple!

The actors wore very fine costumes but there wasn't much scenery then. William would write lines to help the audience imagine where they were.

More about The Globe Theatre

Theatres now are nearly all under cover, but in William's time they were mostly open air. There is a reconstruction of The Globe close to where the original once stood. In Stratford, the Memorial Theatre is dedicated to performing Shakespeare's plays all the year round.

Some important dates in William Shakespeare's lifetime

1564 William is born in Stratford-upon-Avon, England.

1576 The first English theatre opens in Shoreditch, London.

1582 William marries Anne Hathaway.

1583 His first child, Susanna, is born.

1585 His twins, Hamnet and Judith, are born.

1587 William leaves for London.

1588 The Spanish Armada is defeated.

1589 William starts work on his first play, Henry VI, Part I.

1596 Hamnet dies.

1597 William buys his house, New Place.

1599 The Globe Theatre opens on the south bank of the river Thames.

1603 Elizabeth I dies. James I takes over the throne.

1610 William retires to New Place.

1611 William finishes *The Tempest*, the last play written on his own.

1613 The Globe burns down – and is rebuilt.

1616 William dies on 23 April, aged fifty-two.